# Feast of Grace

# Feast of Grace

## Psalms and Poems of the Ordinary Around Us

William Herman

RESOURCE *Publications* · Eugene, Oregon

FEAST OF GRACE
Psalms and Poems of the Ordinary Around Us



Resource Publications
An Imprint of Wipf and Stock Publishers
199 W. 8th Ave., Suite 3
Eugene, OR 97401

www.wipfandstock.com

PAPERBACK ISBN: 979-8-3852-7249-5
HARDCOVER ISBN: 979-8-3852-7250-1
EBOOK ISBN: 979-8-3852-7251-8

VERSION NUMBER 02/04/26

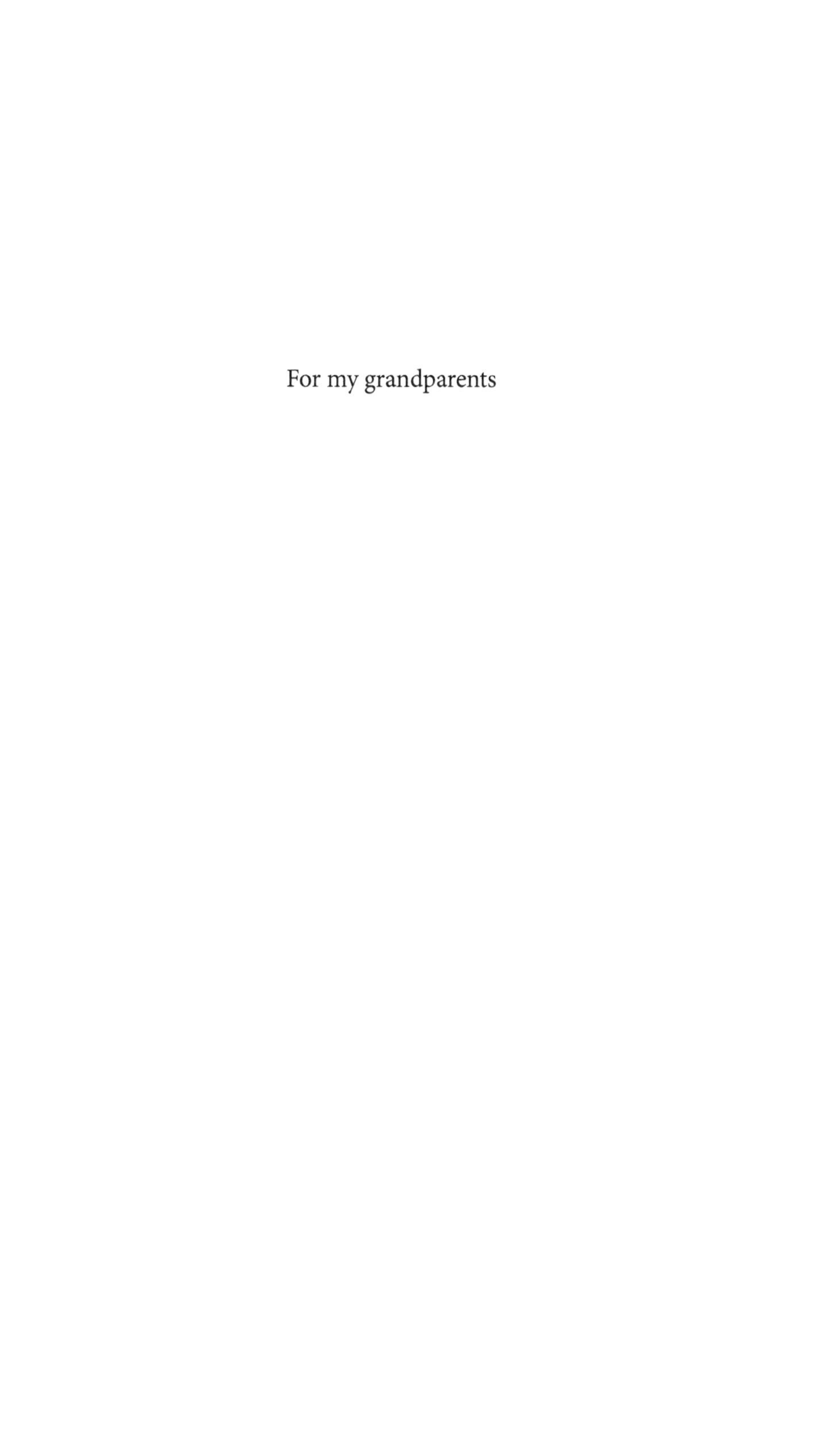

For my grandparents

## Contents

## Mallard Lane Psalm

Something here is foundational to me
As if the sound of leaves as they drift down
Calls out, or sunlit sparkling frost-mist gleams
A sign, or my life-breath that swirls around
Made visible would house some secret part
Of me; one pillar in the basement holds
The architectural Creator's art
Once ruined only now to be made whole.

The Maker made this knowing it would fall
But knowing too that I'd be here one day.
The Builder built this knowing it would call
One holy heart and stir it to His praise.
He's broken down the walls—the cornerstone
Stands, even as the ruin's overgrown.

## Boston in December (BL)

Breath comes in waiting
Early at the bus station
This plume of thoughtful

Epiphany. I
Radiate cold in the cold,
Yankee that I am,

Sleepily waiting
On my breath made visible.
Gathering grey light

Sympathizes with
Out-let exhalation in
Raggedly grey clouds.

Ceding to surprises, I,
On board, am invisible.

## A Psalm of Gold, Cold, & Kings

A silver-bearded oak, old forest king,
Alive and aging, sheds like tears gold leaf
And brown, the pure and dross cast off. He brings
His sylvan joy, his anvil-hammered grief,
To pray, to curse the loss, to join the stones
That cry out—emerald, ruby, amber. Gold
Leaves with the sound and glimmers as it's blown
Amidst the acorns growing in the mold
By gusts of ancient Time delighting in
The Frost who leaves the silver-bearded oak
Grey-white and bare. But ancient Time must spin
His days until the Ancient King revokes
The Tale of Time: the Frost shall lose its cold
And aging shall reverse as brown turns gold.

## Petrichor Joy

After the storm a fresh and windswept sky—
The cloudy souls have ceased their tears—
The pearls in opalescent puddles lie.
Let joy arise! Clouds tear and disappear.
The hope is bright, we passionately wait
For bittersweet, the song we sing, to change
To melodies, to gemstones, blooms, and rays
Of joy that dawn most glorious after rain.
White lilies glow like diamonds from the hope
Reflected in the tiny rippling seas.
Each petal's scintillation fills the scope
Of joy refined and sung in harmony.
As we gaze upward on a sapphire sky
We wait and lift our song: let joy arise!

## Adoration I (for A.R.F.)

O Lord, I come before You trying
To give You back the words You've given me
But nothing I can do will match dying
As sacrificial Lamb, not though I be

A martyr for Your cause and give up all,
Not though I write and sing for all my days,
Or pray with all the zeal of blessed St. Paul,
Or if with David all my psalms I raise.

Lord, even then my debt would be too deep
With all my praise, I still fall short, but Your
Great sacrifice has height and depth to keep
The cup You've given me brim-full and more.

## All the Diamonds (for Oma & Opa)

As ocean scintillation, sun on sea,
Or as the glow of color as light wakes,
So Your heart shines, begetting dawn in me:
The morning of my soul as it might break
As some great bird who's free and now has flown
Or as a soul who from earth's chains is freed
So soars my heart which is no more my own
But trapped within this bruised and broken reed.
As woodland green tranquility subsumes
Me, or as wind amidst the leaves finds rest,
So my heart finds the peace that He of whom
Creation sings has placed within my breast.
O in this light, this flight, this peace I long
To join the earth in scintillating song.

## Poetry & Bacon (for Caleb)

On a small, grey, stir-crazy Tuesday morn
I learn to breathe repentance out and in:
To exhale small, grey sorrow and adorn
The passing day with joy-worn oxygen,
Then to inhale and bare my soul to you
In poetry and bacon. Come evening,
The Spirit moves in sunsets just askew,
Reflected in the cracks and cracklings
Of Tuesdays, filling up the puddles of
Our humanness. I cross myself and think
That we don't count the seconds when we love
Or sleep, and pray for breath between the chinks
Of everydays spent smiling in a dream
And midnights aching for the dreams to come.

## Calling Out Your Name

Beware the fury in a finch's wings,
The rocks' fell voices as they cry aloud;
Beware the clouded song the lightning sings,
The cry the wilderness has been endowed.
For they call only when our song has ceased—
When all mankind has turned idolatrous,
Turned full away and walked to Eden's east—
So cursed will be those days because of us.
In hopeless dark and flame our minds will roam
To wander further into apathy
The cutting voices call to us "go home"
Let Christ return before that day may be.
By grace while we draw breath, oh let us sing
While we are not yet home let praises ring.

## The Lawn

The heartsick soul can find its rest
And so the weary man
Caged or catlike, quick to believe,
The hungry soul can rest.

Ticklish turns of a worn-out road
Smile, grimace, and try to
Teach too much the tempting wayside
Along the weary road.

Blocked and battered by the living,
Afraid to be breathing;
Five miles past the back of nowhere,
Learn to love the living.

Ignore the incurious jays—
Is the limit the sky?
Or the canopy of maples
Inside your irises?

My bold moments creep up on me
Heart heavy as I am
Moving unexpectedly near
In moments far from me.

Here the underbrush chaos fades
Retreating to regroup
Somewhere thirty yards away
To plot vengeance and fade.

Green grass pervades despite the grey,
To protect the stillness,
That solemn spirit of growing
In the golden and the grey.

Leading freely to the road's end
The lawn has no secrets
Yet looks away and laughs alone
For the secrets it keeps.

## Psalm of Linden and Fir (for AG)

You notice much in the moments
When you entertain Silence
And dance with Stillness:

Some fool has carved out
His heart into the wood
Of a sorrow-laden linden.

If you embrace the holy
Quiet, you can hear
The worms devouring the dust

Of your ancestors.
You too will be flames
Of mist and burn away.

Amongst the fallen needles,
You become
The confidant of firs,

The spiders' secret
Keeper of webs and dew,
And solitary maker of cairns.

The modest mushroom will not
Come before you bared
'Til you have known her mistress, Time.

The firs and lindens entwined
Make lovers' boulevards for
The worms and honeysuckle.

As the mist dissipates
And the lawn grows too
Tired to remember to flirt

With you and Time,
The roots that burnt their way
Out of your mind are torn

Up and left like so many
Tongues of flame or worms.
These moments are brief

When you look into the soul of Silence
And dance in Stillness' arms
In the lindens and the firs.

## Maple Psalm (for Mom)

A maple lives by grace in the woodlands
Reaching up by the green forest's meadow,
Beside half a dozen others it stands
Many miles far from tilled earth or hedgerow.
Through many years of everchanging moons
Its leaves and dreams have grown, only to change
As summer turns autumn, morn becomes noon,
Calm precedes storming, and winds rearrange.
Still the tree revels in sunlight and rain
Whispering wisdom to all who pass by;
Breezes flow not through its branches in vain
But with the rocks sing harmony to cry:
"May all I am, so little though it be
Praise the God who cares for the sparrow and me."

## Morning Glory Psalm (for Mary)

There's a hill nearby where blueberries grow
With raspberries and copses of granite
That greet the first light's joy from far below
The heavens and the cumulus that flit
Like strands of morning glory on the hill
That thrives amidst the brambles unafraid
Of soaking in the fate of dawn, the still
And shadowed glory of the unknown day.
At sunrise listen with your nose and eyes
To simplicity and grandeur of light
Incarnate in the soft pink-purple cries
Of flowers that, with berry-like delight,
Lift up their aromatic melody
In scent-song of heaven's resplendency.

## Beech Psalm (for Jack)

I wish to be a tree
Allowing rays of light between my leaves
Living, breathing
Rooted deeply but free
A foretaste of a greater world to be
Branching, towering.

## Oak Psalm (for Anne)

It sways with the wind
The roots hold fast.
Growing and stretching
It bends until it groans
The roots hold fast.
Sparks and icicles
Branching every which way
The roots hold fast.
Black scars of lightning
Bole, bark, boughs, buttresses
In tempest and drought
In whirling hate and rain
The roots hold fast.

## Willow Psalm (for Dad)

The baby mourning doves above the door
Have shyly slipped out from their mother's wing;
The empty nest is home for doves no more,
Just all the dust and moments time will bring.
The willow's fronds grow long down by the creek
Which flows on, never ceasing, evermore.
Beneath are stones; above the sky is bleak.
The doves cry out their mourning and explore
The frame of space and time God's given them.
Their seconds differ somehow from the willow's—
Which takes its time to grow up at the hem:
Eternity's rough edge with time below.
The birds will die, the tree will fall and rot,
The creek and sky will end, but God will not.

## Patience Is the Theme (for Disko)

No one expects the gruesome patience
Of missing your dead dog,
Not in the cold March morning mist
Of walking out from home;
The violent patience wrestling
With God, the maddening
Wait at the door, the peering through
The keyhole at the thread
Eternity is woven with;
And nor does anyone
Expect the hideous patience
Of waiting to be wed
Wrapped in a sweater like a hug
The moment just before
You knew you needed it, and held
By post-cold-rain-walk tea
That smells like chocolate and romance.

## Nights Like This

I walked right by her tears that melted in
The rain and filled my heart but did not flood
My eyes or mind. I felt the trickle, thin
And menacing, of fear erase the good.
Now two years later, almost back at camp,
My mind is racing, fending off the cold:
I could have listened, could have whispered lamp
Light to the rain-blind windows of her soul.
Two pairs of downpour eyes got tangled up
In grace that night, apart and set alone.
The thought of what I could have said disrupts
My nights, like this, when storm and tree intone
Her name in words like whispers just too far
To hear except to wonder what they are.

## The Burning

I'm awake, aren't I?
For the dream ended before
I woke my conscience.

My sin was standing
On ground yet too holy for
Mortal feet and hands.

Something was burning
Besides my throat as it thirsts
For the wet of dew.

It was burning time
Which woke me to the wildness
Of reality

The burning of mind and soul
Against the heart and body.

## Broken Sonnet

There are no waves crashing against this frame.
The water's static. It submerges me
Asphyxiating, drowning as the force
Of pressure builds and presses, weighing down
My chest. There's no dynamic liquid flow.
The water's still and stagnant as it fills
My lungs to bursting. Bronchi writhe about
In suffocation. They can't breathe or pray
As gravity pulls harder on my mass.
My eyes grow wild as I sink wide and deep.
As gaseous air recedes my limbs begin
To twitch and die. The full lack of control
Drives one mad. I abhor, I despite it.
And still that unquenchable joy.

## A Kind of Thorn (for Quincy)

My lips drew breath and opened to the world,
Which offered me delicious thoughts and fresh
Ideas, its baited hook to touch and curl
And penetrate my epiglottal flesh.
The first sensation hurts, but not too much:
The pain is overwhelmed by tasting of
The whole of what I think I feel, and such
A tangled mess of all I say I love.
Enamored with endorphins I recall
The warmth that flooded through my viscera
As dopamine's sweet kiss; I'm too enthralled
To feel that blood flows down my trachea,
Through my esophagus into my bones
And seeps down from the hook to fill all space.
It drowns my nerves, it blinds my rods and cones
Until I'm full with no room left for grace.
The hook has bled me dry, and I may die
Before it's taken out but I will pray
To have the hook ripped out that I may try
To be filled up with blood-bought love and pain.

## Bifurcated Sonnet

Communal room of
A family brought near
To joy and high love
That holds the light dear
And bright resounding
Of home that comes and
Despite the fading
Hopes in the spark fanned
To full bright fire
That makes us fearless
Of all that's higher
Or lower than this
This body mind soul
Our lives are made whole

hiding is enough
to the house of fear
and the mourning dove
through the window's clear
picture of that thing
which we cannot stand
to the dark we bring
into flame the plan
of our dark desire
making nothingness
in our muddy mire
den of hateful mess
heart of blackened coal
of darkness and cold.

## Milk, Honey, Gall

Is it covenant blood before me?
I glance down at my hands,
sheltered in my Dunsinane
My Jericho. It is not.
Yet still it stains my palms
In my periphery. Am I, then,
To see those apparitions and
Stand firm, as Jerusalem,
And run mad having seen
What I have seen? Unsex me here,
O Muse, wash off what I am;
Cleanse me with Neptune's and Jordan's
Souls.

## Psalm of the Wife of Hosea

You find me here amidst what I have craved,
Surrounded by the precipice of crimes
Indelicate. I slither to this cave
Of sooty flame and prostitution grime
And find the stony walls too smooth to touch,
Their curves and edges leading me away,
Debauched to Earth's deep bowels where I clutch
At echoed groans as every lover's prey,
And find You here amidst what I have craved,
The truth of pleasure, not the barren womb
Of brothel bed. You write my name, engraved
Upon the ring of walls, no more the room
Of my betrayal but the soft delight
Of human joy upon the wedding night.

## Sturm und Drang (for Ella)

I stood beneath the trees, wild as the sea
In the maelstrom of the wind and my mind
Allowing stormlight to darken in me
Until the sky's tears fall and mix with mine.
I knelt in the brambles and torrential oaks
My face in the mud of the dust whence I came
'Til peace like a raincloud left my soul soaked
And love drenched me through as well as the rain.
I lay on my back as clouds cleared for light
Warmth flowing through me as sun 'twixt the boughs
As though reminding me that all is right
Despite the wilderness of tangled rout.
Little robin redbreast hops fearless by
A sweet reminder the Lord hears my cry.

## Interstate Psalm (for Lydia)

Suddenly you find yourself on a turn:
A stretch of road with naught but summer's green,
A solitary mind that time has worn,
And wondering what the loneliness could mean.
Driving, alone with your thoughts, in the car
Looking through windshield and rearview mirror
and all you see are yellow lines and tar.
Endless, nothing looks closer or further
Except the mountains, veiled in mist ahead,
The climbs you'll have to make some time not far
From now. But now, you follow as you're led
Along the sometimes empty road. The hard
Grey line winds onward, turning in the green
And hoping for the loneliness to mean.

## Route 116 (for Kaylynn)

It should have been an island and it is
In some strange twist of February's whim:
A frozen silver blinded by the kiss
Of Northern Maine. The river flows its hymn,
Invisible beneath the bridge and ice
As if to sanctify the separate isle
In hypothermic grace. It will suffice
For now to wait—delay the kiss and smile
With urgency and not with haste. The thoughts
Of spring stay sacred, but without a sound.
What should not be an island and is not
Is twisted in the February ground.
(But when the time for spring comes, do not wait)

## Particles of Speech

We talk of participles, poems, and words,
Words, words but lose among them what we mean
By nouns and verbs the Ghost bestows, but stirred
Incomprehensibly in labyrinthine
Novellas, essays, plays, law, treatise, verse,
Subjunctives, prepositions, hyponyms,
Encouragement, injustice, freedom, curse,
Beliefs, absurdities, regrets, and hymns
That deliquesce to ululating cries
Of cold, debilitating nullity
And irrecondite, sophomoric sighs
Until we learn emitting silence frees
Our souls to let the Holy Spirit groan
The prayers we cannot offer on our own.

## Adoration II (for Kylie)

She plays the old, out-of-tune piano
And thus prepares her heart to meet the Host,
To pray redemption on the breath that blows
And carries her beloved, battered notes.
Then to the chapel's stones and wooden beams
Beneath the image of the Cornerstone
The crucified Lord Christ whom it would seem
Has died for good, but He will still atone
And as Christ rises so shall she rise too.
He cried out to the wind, "Forgive them, Lord,
For they know not what work We have to do."
So she comes here to glorify the Word;
"I come to kneel before You and adore;
I know that long before I was, You are.

## Autumn Dreams

It's been four falls already since I came
Here, and the autumn has made all the leaves
A subtle hint of cold. It's not the same
This year, for now they wave farewell from trees
Whose roots go deep and keep them steady on
In one place all their sylvan lives which may
Last for two hundred years or more when gone
Am I, when long is past the autumn day
I walked along the road and chose a leaf,
A brilliant red, and placed it in my coat
To keep it as I helped a friend whose life,
As it has touched mine and departs, denotes
The changing of the seasons, changing green
New life to red to brown to memory.

## Sylven Seasons (X)

I. Spring
Fresh buds and flowers
New life grows upward
Emerging from grey
On the forest floor
All erupts in green
As we walk onward
The ceaseless journey

II. Summer
Laughter fills the air
Full, joyous, complete
Warm and cheerful light
Fills the forest floor
In lazy sunshine
But Time's too busy
To stop and converse

III. Autumn
Bright hues and vibrant
Set the leaves to song
But leaves fall to earth
To the forest floor
Leaves given new worth
Set the path to walk
'Til the end of time

IV. Winter
Falling snow comes down
Traveling to earth
White, cold, silent
On the forest floor
A path, cold, silent
Traveled by mankind
'Til they're given crowns

## A Storefront Windowpane

*In homage to Gerard Manley Hopkins*

Where the wild West Wind twists and twirls
Its serpentine self, worries and hurries and whirls,
Intricate hoarfrost freezes drops
Of future petrichor that stop
Me; I freeze in time-space as the frost
Intimates its fleeting frost-thoughts
Mostly of December crisp cold snow accrued
In mounds around of perennial pulchritude.

Mixing my life-time with the miniscule
Dappled details of criss-cross branching rules
Bends my busy bustling efficiency
Until the West Winds catty-corner-carry,
Wild, whirling, wintry as they are,
Carry it across the world and far
And command I cannot continue or go
On without a stop or walk amidst the snow.

Hectic hurry, wheedling worry whisper-
Scream prophetic profanities but shiver
As intricate winsome hoarfrost wields
Unwittingly a cold steel sword that yields
To world-wise ease, convenience, nought—
Only to the complex simplicity of frost-fraught-thought:
A Christ-Creator capable of unfurling
Frost and wintry souls frozen in the whirling.

## Windows to the Home

In the bittersweet cold of gloaming
I imagine the house from the outside,
My separate self peering in from the falling
Of reflected light distilling itself in precise
Drifts against the clapboard bulwarks of home.

The eyes, half mine, see only in
The half-light, half-truth; the walls,
Two-faced and ideologically thin,
Are real. Only silence pierces, instills,
Drifts, through the panes and sills of home.

I imagine twin candles peering out
Of a fiery body in the apple tree,
Or its spirit, never allowed
Or welcomed in. Still, it can see
Itself in the woodstove of our home.

We keep the spare dreams in the attics
Of ourselves, gently jumbled in boxes
That huddle together against the thick
Cold, inanimate and unstill. I ask
The house aloud, what makes you home?

## Psalm by the Kennebec

Meandering I walked down to the edge
In steps I'd taken often times before,
Allowing the stillness to drive like a wedge,
To split my hardwood ways down to the core.
And with his axe in hand, the woodsman comes,
Intently searching for the perfect tree—
The blade rings true, the trunk's wood gently hums—
Full sure of what his masterpiece will be.
He carves with care; each stroke is made in love,
The wood must decrease as its purpose grows:
Cleaved tight to what it's for not what it's of,
The life it's given, not the one it chose.
I walked along the edge of the ravine
Content to trust his axe and all it means.

## The Colors of Love (for Grace)

A mirror shatters on the cold, hard ground,
A thousand diamonds worthless as the dust,
The shards akin to thorns to make a crown
As sharp as nails, made red with blood and rust.
Yet such as these make windows of stained glass:
A fragment broken for a higher call,
The glass made void of purpose now recast;
Such is the aching beauty of it all.
A mirror shattered far beyond repair,
A thousand pieces placed with care and sealed.
The hues of Noah's rainbow all declare
The glory of the Lord will be revealed.
The sunlight through the stained-glass window shines
And patchwork colors glorify the Light.

## A Myth (BL)

Out in the void where stars like holy fires
Rhythmically flow in nebulaic dance
Opulent in their glorious attire,
Esoteric ideas our thoughts supplant—
Primeval memories we call subconscious
Invade the independence we hold dear.
Galling, the idea there is more than us—
Secretly wondering, we lend them an ear.
Tens of thousands of lightyears far from here,
Ragged, the edge of the universe cries
Nagging the inhabitants of earth to hear
All Heaven's praises refuting the lies.
The glory of the stars shouts, resplendent,
God made man desperately dependent.

## Fire of Paradox (for Sarah)

O God of fiery glory share Your blaze
And teach each candle Your exquisite pain;
Ignite in us the embered wounds of grace
That marked us saved and emptied out Your veins.
O God transcendent You are imminent
Our woodstove Father and our scorching King
A holiness that burns magnificent
A comfort in old scars, illumining
The hearthstone of the heavens, in which leap
The kindled flames of Christ, God in man's frame,
And of the Father, playful, vast, and deep,
And with them glints a wind and tongues of flame.
All three are comfort for our cold, hard selves
And cleansing fire keeping us from Hell.

## Going Upta Camp

Have you seen geese that glide across the moon
In white, a V-shaped, late-night dance up high?
Or have you heard the lonesome cry of loons
And listened to the lake's far shore reply?
Through icicles watch as the sun goes down:
A thousand broken glimmering rays rebound.
Or listen to the wind in leafy crowns
And hear the song of worship in the sound.
The deep and breathing green of conifers,
The sun reflected in the ocean's blue,
The snowflakes white in innocent splendor;
Surprises mixed in all creation's hues.
Like loons' lost cries, creation's echoes ring
A song to its Creator crowned the King.

## An Artist I

The artist writes his grace-notes in the curves
And almost-lines that harmonize as words,
A gathering of flowers, undeserved
Beside the image of a maker blurred
By discord. Beautiful still, in its way
Of unexpected ordinary forms
And rhyme—a body and a work at play.
The poet makes the composition warm:
Alive, and real, and yet imperfect. Art,
Desire, and healing in the melody
Of simple function married at the start
To meaning's undertones. A poetry
Of grace is written. The composer makes
His music, his creation, come awake.

## An Artist II

A secondary artist, I, as man
Is wont, take up my pen, enamored. I,
In awe and inability to span
A canvas or an octave, I will write
My palette and my key in words which seem
To never be enough yet stretch beyond
Their measure—bend until they almost scream
In agony and pleasure like the sound
Of a piano or the tints of paint
That stretch these earthly frames to understand
Some inkling of the light of grace and taint
Of hate. The words, the sound, the hues demand
Of us our awe and our ability
To form the grace we hear, we think, we see.

## Easter Sunday on the Cay (for Marme)

A group of mostly strangers gathers here
To celebrate the newly risen Son.
The sandy island cemetery hears
And listens to the rooster greet the dawn,
And as the day retrieves her wits and pride,
Our man-made light-post hides its now-dim face.
This momentary half-light coincides
With cloudlace tearing, opening the space
Where mango glow rebirths the deadened sky.
The holes left by the mortal stars are swarmed
With voices welcoming in glad reply
The sun to Calvary and Man-O-War.
We wait until the two expanses break
And they do.

## **Salubrious Amphiguity**

Imagine for a moment
You're amphibian and
Can breathe the rain
So petrichor becomes
Joy *and* life
And you are citizen
Of two worlds, denizen
Of pond and palimpsest.

## A Feast of Grace (for Karis)

O Ordinary Day let me not forget you
Nor glance over you in search of some bright
And ever-elusive Tomorrow
For whom I wait, but waiting is
Its own sort of grace, isn't it? Right up there
With that time I first saw snow on a beach
And gasped in the delicious cold air
Distilled down from the cirrostratus.

O Ordinary Day let me not regret you
Nor fail to see the mercy it was
To simply exist in your embrace,
Warm as the scent of home after hard work
And cold wind, and warm as the flames
Of the candlesticks along the table
As we gather after tromping through underbrush
To taste the last notes of a sipsichor* sunset.

O Ordinary Day let me not pass you by
Nor hurry along, too distracted
To see the moments of grace you've waited
To adorn my hours with, like the leaf-bound bones
Of that creature I found in the back woods and
Like forgiveness when it comes time for broken
Goodbyes and the night dawns anew.
O Ordinary day, let me not forget you.

*Sipsichor: the pleasant, rejuvenating smell of wet leaves turning to leaf-soil in early winter and late spring

www.ingramcontent.com/pod-product-compliance
Lightning Source LLC
LaVergne TN
LVHW010546100826
845148LV00013B/2622
* 9 7 9 8 3 8 5 2 7 2 4 9 5 *